Fuchlestichs

Fuchlestichs

Leon McConnell

Resist Entertainment
2025

Copyright © 2025 by Resist Entertainment

All rights reserved. This book or any portion thereof may not be reproduced or used in any manner whatsoever without the express written permission of the publisher except for the use of brief quotations in a book review or scholarly journal.

First Printing: 2025
ISBN 979-8-9853126-2-1
Resist Entertainment
Boyle Heights, California

Cover Art by Leon McConnell

Bitten Style

From the heart the mouth speaks
It licks its lips
Our hearts used to tangle tongues
And our mouthes would whisper fingers
Through hair that totally
undid all our knots
I feel like I've lost a tooth in you
The way little heart strings
hold on to things
That are falling
Till your mouth spits out the blood
And your tongue reaches
for the empty space
Where we were putting roots down
No one talks about ghosts' teeth
But you promised you'd haunt me
Now all I have is words in my mouth
And a hole in my heart

Today We Mope

You must conjure the world you walk through
You must construct the steps you ascend
out of friends
You must drag walls out of dreams
And bones out of nightmares
And breathe life into the home you inhabit
You must push loved ones off rooves
And sever the hand you're holding

If they can't keep up
Because the world turns fast
And the edge comes quick
You must dive into oblivion
And paint your skin in the blackest tears
You must fall like hope
And let god pierce you
Pick up the bone splinters
And cast a suspension bridge of disbelief
Withoutwards from the cavity your soul
is cowering in
To let life in
Then greet it like the animal you are
Scurrying from the corner
With a shard in your mouth
Shake outreached to say
Hello

Leon McConnell

Riddle

I'm not a spotlight
Not a stoplight
Not a neon, flash, flicker
Moonlight
Reflected in a puddle
I'm no fluorescent recess
No lighthouse
No halo
No iridescent algae
Waiting to
Wash up on your beach
I'm no sun
No reflection
No dream of a dead star
Drift from galaxies away
I'm not static
No gunshot in the dark
No blue spark
This little light of mine

Doesn't turn on
When the refrigerator door opens
I'm no lamp in a smoky room
No vending machine
Saying it's out of cigarettes
I'm not the pinprick of hope in a collapse
I'm no sign
I'm a match lit briefly
Burning Through Space and Time
Like detritus on the forest floor

The Human Mistake

What if your soul isn't beautiful at all
What if it's tattered
What if greed is leeches
Siphoning the juice out of you
What if your soul is starving
Its ribs sticking out like speed bumps
Crud barely pumping through
Your little system
Malnourished
What if your soul is deformed
What if it was never pretty
What if you were a mistake
What if your soul is a cockroach
in the gutter
Fed a diet of child pornography
A tyrant screaming willing to hurt
Anyone in a whim
What if we just say souls are beautiful
Because we want humanity to have
Some value
Some unity
What if some souls have no soul at all
That'd seem pretty human to me.

Naptime

Most days, I'm aiming for a beauty in the void, to conjure some celestial gift, to trade the magic in my marrow for a speck of glee, a tiny shining light, singing songs off god's radio, inhaling pure joy and exhaling some contention. But today, I'm begging for the void to pull me under, to cover me deep deep miles down in a charcoal blanket grave. Today I'm begging to disappear, from time, from humanity. Today I pray the void absorbs me. And I pray that I can wake up someday pulled from this vomit back to life and reaching for some great yellow orb, playing shadow puppets in the sky.

Our Cozy Home

To flirt with a poltergeist is one thing
One flirts with excitement
One fucks excitement
Takes a road trip with it
Drifts away and is vaguely haunted
By dishes thrown across the kitchen
But to get to know the ghost
The pulse of its temper
The incantation hidden in everyday phrases
That summons its maelstrom

Is a fool's undertaking
You can no more graft a garden to your side
Than you can grow hand in hand with someone
Who inhabits a tiny corner of hell there next to you

Stretched

Only my sisters who've taken a cleaver to the
heart know how deep my scars run
Somehow this dead tissue is beating
as life glides above it
The way a poltergeist
is an energy echoing
A time trapped in space
Spirits echo in my body
Death echoes
Sometimes I feel possessed
by their stories
And I have to replay them
But it's just energy
Pulsing in psychic wounds
You touch me
And don't even feel that
Your fingers don't run over my brain
Scarred memories
And my heart is intangible
A valley for you
Forever reaching

Second Moon

Sometimes the neighborhoods I carry, the dead who follow, the universes I've stumbled through, the planets inside of me, they weigh a little heavy. Life squeezes a little tighter. And God is a moth in the bathroom, camped out for a week, watching how I'll handle the pressure.

Will I blow up? Annoyed at a loved one. Pestered by their digging. This whole electric everything lives inside me from the first forever I've ever heard mentioned down to the last breath of holy lepidoptera beating at my window, begging to be protected from the Mojave Desert's one hundred degree luna.

Sensible

I can't give you any depth because it's hard to hold together eternity. It's hard to answer your questions about today when I remember every blood cell fluttering through Los Angeles 1984 in the back of a Ford Pinto, the Night Stalker terrorizing us all, Sydney stained with scum debris 1999 from a taxi cab, an Iowa farm in 1935 burning, the slave ships, god's first baby plucked from his very own belly, wondering what anything is, one thousand eyes full of angel dust. I'm just trying to hold it all together and not get crushed between the ghosts' breath you call dark matter. Please forgive me. Most of the time I'm very sensible.

The Less of Us

The me outside of me
Living in the hearts, minds and memories
Of people I've touched is being culled
It's not that I'm isolating
So much as I'm being removed
Like dead skin
Or once loved neighborhoods
Time just takes us away
And when I call out to myself
The answer back
Is less of a heartbeat
And more of a dream
A nap dream
You definitely had it
But who can remember what it was
And your day goes on anyway
So I just continue on my own
The one me
And the less of us
Floating towards a dune to rest
Settling in to this desert afterlife
No encore
Burnt out and alone
Like stars in the sky

Flower

Compartmentalizing
Is a shifting of one's vital center
Minimizing what you touch
And what touches you
Because a danger
Has come for your control
A hurt can be infectious
Traveling towards the core
Black veins of poison
This is why i cut you off
To save my heart
From breaking
I'm holding on to life
In smaller increments
Deeper fingers
Greater force
Folding in
Me unto me
Closer & Closer

Tolerance

You get used to anything
Motorcycles and vines
Shanties and humidity
McMansions and air-conditioning
Homeless people shitting on the sidewalks
Corruption and ignorance
Deer towers and subzero wind chill factors
Car rust shitty food
Tacos sushi pizza
Bomb sex
Your girlfriend crying
The smell of aluminum burning
Your dog slowly forcing you off the bed
Some tiny sanctuary
Changing countries
Praise fat paychecks
Bruises
A few drops of blood
Hate and dead bodies
Love
Lovelessness
Wasting time
Lives wasted
Praise
And the grace of God
War
Way too much

On the Cusp of a Null Arbor

The most perfect perfect
I've ever walked through
Was getting dropped off somewhere
at a crossroads in the middle of nowhere
Just as dark was walking in
and setting its bag down
I could have lived there
This lost memory of planet earth
Could've swallowed me
But I grabbed the sun
As she was walking out the door
Risking my fingers in the process
And before the taste of daylight
Ebbed from my lips
A ride came
And drove me
A continent away

Fuchlestichs

Human People Things:

Mark Hemphill

After my grandmother died. My uncle got a little money from Social Security, and he bought this SUV, and he had this pretty little Italian girlfriend, Jennifer. It didn't last too long, but I admire that he was trying to find some happiness. I remember them talking about wanting to go be park rangers somewhere, a tweeker and a junkie… just riding the wave.

My uncle had so many other stories. So many chapters. That was one of his last. He didn't make it too long after his mother passed. They were bound together in codependence and abuse. But before homelessness, HIV, and just checking out, before his young book was closed, before the car got totaled and the girl left, he found a bright spot there in the dark. I like stories like that, stories about the wave's crest before it crashes. I think those are the most human stories and human is the most we can be.

Grethel Peralta

Poverty is dirty but Neces's house was clean. The inside smelled like lavender Fabuloso. It was stark, and minimalist. The outside was graffiti whitewashed in sunshine. Every fucking inch of it. Names scrawled on cacti, etched into every corner. I guess that's why inside was spotless. She lived next to the American Motor Inn. Prostitutes spilled out onto Long Beach Blvd. My grandfather owned a gas station a block away from there before I was ever born. The ruins of the place sat there long past my teens.

Neces was more than just the pin-up of our little scene. She was respected. She grinded. She had skills. Being who I was granted me keys to the city. I was not respected. I like to think I grinded. But I didn't really have skills. Luckily though, my cousin was a big shot in juvenile crime. So, nepotism paved my way into this backyard graffiti Mecca, hosted by a minor tagging superstar. We all thought it was weird she had such a German name. Grethel. She looked really Guatemalan. You know in the way sometimes Guatemalans might look a little Asian. In my wandering, sometimes I'd be alone on Tweedy and pass through all the crack heads in the triangle off State Street and head back to familiar territory. I'd just end up there on her steps. She'd bring me inside. Her sister would make chicken soup and we'd sit and watch horror movies. Even if her boyfriend showed up, no one cared. I was Time's cousin. I was harmless. Sometimes we'd talk about Jesus or drugs. She was obsessed with Candyman. Once in a while we'd stroll Martin Luther King Boulevard with dusk approaching. I'd carry her on my back. Happy to have a friend.

Nowadays I don't know what happened to her. Everyone from Lynwood and South Gate is gone. Someone said she became an art professor. She was always more arty than the rest of us. We were hoodlums, criminals, kids just running the street. Adventurers. I never go back there. I hate passing through ghosts. But still, I'm haunted and ghost stories just spill out of me.

Divorce

You know what was nice? When I got divorced and the only thing I had built in my life was a complete wasteland, just utterly destroyed. I would get in my car and wander, just drive with no shore to reach. Just drive and listen to the music and watch the scenery. Who knows where the fuck I'd end up, Anza Borrego, or a field in the middle of Ventura County, Wilmington. It didn't fucking matter. I just had to drive because I felt destroyed and nothing helped but looking out the window as the world passed me by. Now, I've smelled the necks of countless strangers and I know there's no alchemy in human bodies or spirits that will fix my life. I've been to the farthest outerlands and hidden gardens walled in a labyrinth tucked away in the palm of god yet despite the magic I know exists in places and men, no enchantment will build a staircase and move my legs up out of the hole that is life. There's nowhere to go.

Smile

I recently learned that not everyone grows up the way you did. It's a strange thing to learn. My family's from South Gate, a suburb of Los Angeles about seven miles southeast of downtown. Some people think it's ghetto. Some people say it's working class. Some people think it's nice. It just depends on your point of view. Anyway, I took tennis lessons as a kid. And sometimes we had toast for dinner. I went to private school sometimes but often we didn't have a car. Everything was a struggle all the time, depending on what this one young woman could do with what she had and what she was up against. She didn't have much and she had a lot against her but I marvel at what she pulled off. I guess what I'm trying to say is, you don't know where people are coming from or what they've experienced or what that cost. So, be supportive, be open, be kind. Yes, I grew up in a household with a heroin addict, but I also grew up in a household with a tennis pro and a lot of people would say I'm from the ghetto but for all my achievements, I'm pretty much the least successful member of my family. And I'm a happy mfukka so, that's worth a smile at least.

When You Took Advantage

One time I was at Melody Lounge with my very good friends Kristian and Lauren, and it just so happened that it was some random girl's birthday, and the bartender gave us all shots and the girl got super drunk and threw up in the bar. This was like 6pm on a Tuesday by the way. They threw her out, but she ran into the street and almost got hit by a car. We all heard the screech and turned our heads. Meanwhile I was making out with some lady at the bar, and she was wasted so I walked with her to a fancy Chinese food restaurant that I would never go to myself because I don't really care for Chinese food, I just didn't want this person who's tongue i just swallowed to find her way into danger incoherent. And since I wasn't hungry, once I saw that she wasn't gunna pass out on the street, I bounced. A couple days later, I invited her to go camping with me & Kris, since he was from Denmark, had never been to LA and was keen on checking out the desert. They don't have those in Europe. But now, in the soberside world she said I took advantage of her. I was like what? I was drunk too. How is two drunk people kissing at a bar taking advantage? Anyway, she didn't come, and I never spoke to her again, but I think she follows me on Duolingo.

A few days after that Kris and I were in Joshua Tree just wandering through the random nothingness. We were way off the road, exploring some small rock gulch oasis dirt formation when we found a teeny tiny coffin buried inside a pile of rocks in a cave. It looked like some spooky voodoo shit, and it had my sister's name written on it. Which creeped me out. The next day we went to El Centro and looked in pawn shops. Then Blessing, an artist I met as a small child at a music festival in line with her mother took us to a punk show in a thrift shop where we saw some Japanese band touring Mexico and we met Skyla who would go on to be in my music video and roam the northwest. Our trip ended the next morning once we ate lots of pancakes at ihop which Kristian thought was as American as life could ever be, and it was.

Note on the Side of the Road

I've been picking up hitchhikers when I can find them. It's not so easy anymore. Yesterday I picked up Levon outside a bathroom in a national park.

I thought he was 30 years old, but he was an 18-year-old kid, just one with a full beard. He seemed to have a good head on his shoulders. I wish him all the best making his way out there, living in a sleeping bag on holiday in public restrooms the way only an 18-year-old could.

Today I picked up Paul from the middle of nowhere on the side of the road in Central Oregon. He's in tune with the earth the way someone like me could tell you what's happening in the NBA. Also, he seemed at least a little crazy. Maybe a little bit more than a little. I thought he was in his 70s but he was in his mid 50s. A former skateboarder from Orange County with deep weathered wrinkles crossing his visage. How do you get from skating pools in SoCal to dodging wolves and avalanches? Perhaps by sleeping too close to the river a few times too many. Life takes us crazy places.

Sugar Fat Tears

There's still tiny flecks of paint near the shower where you painted a wig fluorescent yellow several years ago. I spot them as I dry off but am evicted from my hypnotic train of thought by the homeless man who lives in the parking space beneath my bathroom window. He's smoking and setting off m80s, which triggers car alarms. He's kinda my neighbor and a little more than homeless since he used to live next door even though now, he lives in a car because they towed away the work van he'd stolen and lived in for several years. I guess he cheated on his wife and she kicked him out. Years later he came back. Now he just works on cars he'll never fix underneath my bedroom. His cigarettes annoy me. I should probly scrub your wig paint away.

Question Mark

Who knew I'd come home from two years of travel to live in my sister's garage
To watch her oldest son start kindergarten and head off to college on a scholarship
Who knew?
Who knew I'd make friends I love
Who knew I'd start a career as a private investigator and a rap group with Xavier

Who knew I'd live in a crazy house
Find my own place to live, and attempt domesticity
Who knew we'd lose Aaron and Priscilla
Who knew I'd make a friend for life
Who knew my movie would finally come out
That I'd publish three volumes of poetry
And a spoken word album. Who knew?
Who knew I'd start making music on my own
That my whole approach to art would change
That I'd fall in love with my favorite artist
I never saw it coming. Who knew the world would shut down. Who knew I'd quit my job
That my dad would die. That I'd win a luxury car
And a game show and make somebody else's films
Who knew?
Who knew I'd own a home
And write a children's book
And become even healthier. Who knew?
Who knew life was taking us here
And who knows where life is going
It just keeps going
Curves and all

Meadows

The pandemic changed people. Five years ago, I pulled an old friend's tampon out with my teeth. The other day, we were sharing nachos and she got mad that I licked my fingers.

Tom Kha

When I tell you my favorite thing to eat is tom kha, it's understood that I'm required to lie. I can't tell my mom and boring people at dinner parties that my favorite thing to eat in the world is pussy. I eat pussy like true reality can only be found between thighs on the tip of my tongue, on the flat of my tongue, sliding around my fingers till my palm meets the clit. God feeds me. I'll suck the pussy juice out of you like my mouth was on the cusp of something great, starving for evolution. When I plug in, reading you, for the next forty-five minutes we're going to take your body as far as it can go. I'm gunna eat your pussy like it was what god put me on this earth for. Your little quivers, spasms, shakes, the way your clit swells, the way my fingers slide on the ridge inside, running water, tells me that your jet is ready and we're going to pierce the sky. I'm here locked in. You can kick. You can scream. I want you to. I want you to beg for me to stop. I want your boundaries rotten, soaked through, mattress gone. I want to turn your body on when I flip the switch. When I eat you, I want you to know that you've been devoured. And when I leave, It's only cuz my belly's full.

Leon McConnell

HmHm

Most people wouldn't consider themselves animals. They have no empathy. They don't value life. They value *their* life. They don't think of themselves as being closer to a panda than a god. Most people are bumbling twits, nowhere near as cute as pandas. But we're not hiding in caves, running from predators. We've banded together, riding the coattails of smarter animals, animals closer to God, animals preying on life itself. Their momentum, their harnessing the collective humanity, our life force buzzing like an engine driven as fast and as far as it can go, even off the face of the earth, too far to kiss, has left us stranded, stalled in mid-air, looking for a captain.

So, I get virtual reality. I get religion, drug fueled orgies, greed piling dollars bodies high. It's the most human thing we can do. Silly fucking animals, lighting the planet on fire, making up stupid rules, pushing their feet down into the earth till their bones are ground cartilageless to prove a point, to be anything but an animal.

Imagine whales, ants, monkeys, dogs driving to some imaginary chore instead of just being where they are, eating what they eat. Imagine ducks building skyscrapers to house an infrastructure of abstract concepts they've forced all ducks to live by, assigning tasks based on feather width instead of just gliding across a pond. Imagine moths hating moths 7,000 miles away over a difference in opinion and fearing that difference so much they build weapons big enough to destroy the entire planet.

No, we're not animals because no animals would do this. We're worse. We're men.

Wormhole

Things 19 year old me would be happy about:
I have a car (I have three cars)
I have an apartment (with no roommates)
I also own a house
I've had lots of crazy sex
I'm rich (not really, but he would think I am)
I've put out a lot of music into the world
I've put books out into the world
I've traveled around the world
I'm not bald
I have a moustache
I made a feature film
I've made a lot of short films
I've performed a lot as a poet and a musician
I've worked as an actor
I've made money as a photographer
I've had art shows
I don't feel like I've done any one any great wrong
I haven't hurt anyone, not anymore than life's friction dictates as we pass bodies
I didn't go to prison
I didn't become a cop
I didn't become a priest

Leon McConnell

I had a real career, in an odd interesting field
My life has been made, not wasted
I'm not a failure

19 year old me wanted
A girlfriend
He wanted children
He wanted to be spectacular
He wanted to be the brightest light
And for the loneliness to go away
But it doesn't. I can't help that
I don't think I've succeeded
In giving him those things entirely
You trade things. We tried.
I'd love to show him
All the avenues of life
He never considered
How beautiful the interconnectedness
of being can be
He would be amazed
Because he thought he was so smart
But his point of view was so small
Just one myopic body

He would be sad at all the death around us
The broken links you make do with closing
But never truly mend
He would be happy we escaped
Poverty And abuse And drugs And crime
We had to flee the country for that
He would be happy we danced
for years and years, until our body was broken

Fuchlestichs

He would be disappointed
That my Spanish wasn't better
Because its one of the few things
He actually worked hard at learning
And he would hate my taste in music
19 year old me was extreme
He was undiluted
like some purer form of gasoline
He was ready to burn at the thought of fire
In some other timeline
He became just charred countryside

I think he'd like me
I'd like to think I could tolerate him
Most of the time
He was a good kid
He just never had any direction in life
He came from a very particular corner of nothing
Slanted towards oblivion
Nineteen year old me wrote his ideology with razors
Because he couldn't see a future that didn't end in blood.

I'd like to think I could tell him he could trust me
I'd like to tell him I'm working on our ferry tickets
Cuz everything is upstream
And the other side is always almost there
But we got there man
We're really close
Really close

Leon McConnell

ありがとう

Here in Japan where it's winter
The place is so clean
Even the seediest parts of Tokyo
Are immaculate
Once in India, I saw horses in the snow
eating out of the trash
I haven't spoken to anyone
Except the friendly chubby Korean man
In a velour track suit who keeps pushing
Packets of instant coffee into my hand
And apologizing that he can't speak English
We're in Japan
I don't speak Japanese or Korean
No need to apologize
My lil rolly polly friend
Walking around here
Is foreign but it's easy
I feel like I'm in a computer simulation or a dream
I feel like I don't belong here
In the most friendly way
It all moves so easily
I got sick a couple days ago
And haven't eaten for awhile
My head feels so clear
Japan is a sanitarium
This is my glass house on the Austrian Alps
Being removed helps
Taking a break from your conflict

Fuchlestichs

From your struggle
From pushing the boulder up the hill
I feel like I can breathe easier
And not just because Los Angeles is on fire
It's a topia just right for my goldilocks temperament
So busy I stay occupied
So quiet I can think
I feel ready
Ready to move on
Ready to be my best me
Thank you Tokyo

Leon McConnell

Regular Ass Poems:

Math

When you look for the meaning of life
Beyond simply living
You seek to assign a value
Something that can be extracted
Something you can trade this life for
And in creating that equation
Lives that do not add up in trade
To the balance are worthless
But life is just there to live
It's so strangely human
To make it a win or lose situation
With a prize at the end
If you get enough points

Cloth

Dreams are the most stretched thread bare frothy fingertip breaths touching our toes where the deep sea of life fogs mirrors against the sands of time.

Band-Aids

I'm not trying to heal
I'll carry this scar the world over
Like a continental divide
And keep moving forward

Leon McConnell

Grey Skies

There's a place I keep seeing in my dreams
and I don't know if it's real
It's a dance floor on the sea
Out in the middle of nothing
I wonder if anyone's ever been there
Or it's some heaven, waiting just for me

Lot in Life

The shortest distance between two points
Is a dark stretch of highway with no homes
No distractions, no friends
It's a tunnel stuffed full of milky way
A long road through the Mojave
A lost time
And you'll be wrinkled when you come out
There is no bed for you
There is no dog or children
There's just a song you whistle
As headlights are refracted by the windshield
Twisting like a disco ball
So enjoy a smile when it comes
You've got years to go yet

Round and Round

You say the words "I love you"
And maybe you feel it too
But no actions get through
You're a closed loop

Plus One

I am who I am inherently
So I don't need no fucking therapy
You can take what you want from me
But I'll never give you nothing willingly
Shit ain't the way that it ought to be
But I'll never buy into your toxic positivity

An Introduction

Maybe we could go rollerskating sometime
I'd love to watch your hips sway
And grab handfuls of ass as I keep you from falling
Maybe we could land in some nice grass
And peel those little shorts off so I can eat you out
I'd love to leave your legs dripping
And have you skating through puddles

Conversation between Passing Mammals

A man walking through the forest at night
Meets a wolf and he's like
Hey wolf
And the wolf is like
Hello there human
Why are you out so late in the dark?

Well, I started my trip ill-prepared
I'm sore and cold and tired
I don't have any water

Leon McConnell

Would you like me to eat you?

Not today wolf. But thank you

Another time then

Let's hope not

Farewell human
Adios Wolf

Selector

You have to just find a corner of life, a slice
a small section to focus on and care about
Life is too immense
To take the whole thing in with any intensity
Pick a thing

Roam

There's no roads in the wilderness
All the paths you tread
Must be hacked for
And born of skin scraped from your forearms

Theres no friends in the wilderness
If any two rows of teeth doesn't eat you
It's because they weren't starving
as you passed by

Fuchlestichs

Dark Water

I ain't painting a picture
I'm in the cave drawing
These four corners of the night closer
Why pretend there's any presentation
Ima searcher
A lurker
Addicted to dark water
Born out of lies
Nobody's father
At most
I just want to float
Till the winds lift the sails
Then drift away
Rub that out
Slap the erasers together
Then blow the little dust cloud
And walk back to your seat

Ow

I've only ever heard women
Talk about a good pain
But I feel a hurt that makes me happy
When I think of love
Being in love
Wanting love
Thats a good pain
I guess

Aura

All of the cracks in my armor is shining
I wear this suit to protect you
The light from inside me is blinding

Eleven Letters

Abandon all pretense
And enter into the pure ritual
Of touching true life
All eyes all brains
All understanding
Only glimpses
Tiny corners
The infinite to us
Is only fathomed as 11 letters
This symbolic token
Offered by the being
Is what life knows we can understand
We don't even gather
That being is more than life
That being is more than non life
That being is possibility
And possibility is limitless

Look at Me Don't Look at Me

My scars are tender ravines
You can fit your fingers through
Though I don't really like being touched
I like crowds of people, the anonymity
I like being lost in life
I welcome sleep
The nothingness of it
Gives me something to aspire to

Honor Roll

Shout out to you if you're doing something.
Shout out to you for trying.
Shout out to you for having goals
Shout out to you for working towards them

Shout out to you for having boundaries
Shout out to you for defending them
Shout out to you for distancing yourself
From people who don't respect your boundaries
Even if you like them

Shout out to you for caring about yourself
For making it to the gym
Even if it's not as much as you'd like
Shout out to you for making yourself happy
Keep doing it

Shout out to you for considering
That maybe you're wrong
That maybe lots of stuff you think you know
May not be wholly accurate and in tune
With the true true
Shout out to you for being a seeker
For seeking love
And wisdom
And joy
And for always trying to be kind and kinder
I think you're doing a good job

The Meaning of Life

The meaning of life is to share kindness. If you do you will find that you are one, that you are attached to others and that all kindness attaches us, so that in every act of kindness the bonds across existence are strengthened. Life becomes more alive. It is self-defining. Kindness is the highway, the medium and the sustenance throughout which all life feeds, travels and lives.

Yuck

Hate is such an ugly expression
Your disgust radiates
And gives off a fowl chemical
Infecting everyone's air

Origin Story

When you're left on your own
from the time you can walk
That no one truly cares is thee most evident thing
you could ever grasp
Your whole life is lived on your own
The only way you can engage with people
is as a spectacle
This is how I became an artist

Double Down

Who knows what's waiting out there
It could be so much worse than this
Pulling the trigger could be
Waking up from this nightmare life
Into a whole new nightmare reality
Except you can't go back to sleep

Staples

As a writer, fiction is easy. It's one part truth and six parts imagination. Which is really simplifying the matter, because in truth, you're creating a world and filling it with living beings made of letters and the brain's electricity. Writing about myself is harder. I feel like I'm stealing from this life to translate a world into words and that I'm betraying myself by giving anyone any little piece of me they haven't earned with their own breath.

Leon McConnell

Some Advice

Build real true networks of life
Give pieces of your heart to friends
Tell stories, scatter seeds
And grow a human forest of interconnectedness
Fight hard against the downside of your biggest traits
Because these will control you
They should be tempered
Not indulged

Factory Town

If you're unique
You probly won't fit
No circle wants you
Don't wear yourself down
To be a part in the machine
Be the oddly shaped rock
Someone steps on and screams

No Spark Ever

Painted into a corner
I'm at the end of a road
I got a full tank of gas
But got nowhere to go
I might just catch on fire
I might just light a fuse
Maybe I'll expire
Because I'm so tired
And I got so much to do

Pattern Recognition

Having been raised in the culture of chaos
The mates I've chosen are those that I considered
Most likely to carry on what I consider normal

GoodBye

Seven Dimensions removed from my existence
isn't far enough away
I wish you some alternate reality
Where you're dirt, getting eaten and shitted out
By other dirt
Into a sea of dirt sucked into a dirt hole
And burning in a dirt hell
Get away

Self-Realization Fellowship of One

I'm realizing, now that I walk in his house and sit in his chairs, that my dad died because out here in the desert, there's only you. You have to face yourself. There's no distractions. There's nowhere to go and no one to meet. Just you and if you sit here for long enough with yourself, you'll learn who you are down at the core. I think my dad came to realize that he was a horrible person and that broke him.

Leon McConnell

Shoulder

This engine
Driving me
Can't stop
Even as the car breaks down
Even when I'm fucking dead
I imagine
There is no rest

Ghostride the Whip

If we could choose where we haunt
I'd pick the Mojave Desert
I'm sure a lot of people would choose
their family home
Or maybe a bar, a restaurant, a beach
So often my mind is in the desert
This nothing. A stasis
To me the desert is just existing
It's where I stop and take a deep breath
Not that the dead breathe
But I imagine that they see and speak
Despite having no ocular nerves
or real flesh mouths
So maybe they breathe
I like the life that exists in this lifeless place
I choose to spend my afterdeath in the desert

Clawed Out

There's no escape
No magic nook that you can hide away in
There is no missing puzzle piece
You are complete
That doesn't mean you won't be lonely
The blanket that you've been woven into
Traced in strands going back to a fish
Crawling out of the sea
Has followed time's path
To keep you warm through these nights
Now here you are in an alleyway
It's one AM and this rain has you hemmed in
You're a kitten drowning in your parents' overflow
You're the inevitable, a murdered potential
A zombie clawed out of a conclusion
Toxic positivity would end each sentence
In a sunshine smiley face
Self-care, self-healing, self-realization
Are placebos for the weak
False courage, an emperor's bullet proof vest
You will die. You will hurt. You will fail
You will wish you had died sooner
Everyone you thought maybe you could love
has moved on
Like your youth
Pain will become a mildew on your bones

And you'll be forced to imagine
There is a joy in places you never looked
And then your eyes will leave you
You'll have to grope your way to happiness
The blanket that covers you is a swaddling
Your children set you in a womb
Return to mother earth

Wetlands

When you meet these soft denizens
Of the animal kingdom
These polite frogs on a dewy day
They don't see your map
Where you've come from
Or where you're going
They don't see your candle burning
In some dark blue third story night
They don't see your prayers

They don't see the world at your tail
Or the whirlwind in your breath
They only sense the most immediate
In every hello they hear only greetings
Every handshake is just a shake to dewy frogs

Devourer

This thing in you that wants
This starving hunger is a real person
This devourer is a being
Whispering in the ear of every part of you
The ache, the grabber, the greedy one
The plunderer
Is a universe, an inkblot
Darkmattering stardust
Sunk into every surface
Its spores, its tendril
Touch on every facet, and burrow
There's no resistance
RapeLifeDestruction is born here
At the inbetween
The swallower
The ravenous one
Is the shadow on every other side
The harvester who howls in blood
Is calculating and furious
The glutton is there
Unharmed by fire Uncut by razors
What we call want is the electron in every atom
What we call drive is the string
Holding this all together
The finger tying the string
And the hand
Leading the kitten along the floor
For the sake of some amusement

Leon McConnell

Boomerang

Im coming back to echo park
A little more sick and tired
A little more depleted
Hoodie covered in pollen
I've wandered the world over

Im coming back to Boyle Heights
To wipe the soot off my car
And change my locks
To deadbolt the door
And liquidate
Like the blackest caterpillar

Im going back to fort mohave
To act like nothing ever exists
To pour my soul out
It isn't easy
Its like scraping
Blood off of gravel

Im stepping out into the world
Like the angel of death
Amazed at all this
Still living

Colonizer Vacation

Cold Europeans
Walking warm beaches
Spending tiny parcels
Of their stable economies
In old playpens
Their ancestors left
After plundering
To self-govern
Isn't this great
They say
Like aliens probing
Shallow depths

Sometimes a Black Hole is a Thought

I've watched stars burn out in my living room
Unwrapping the tiny gifts they cried over
Bleeding against the wall

Leon McConnell

Telephone

It's a strange thing to learn, and you're not going to get it just because I tell you, God can't be ascertained. There is no point in this lifelong struggle where you succeed. God isn't a video game. God is love given as a gift. You can't earn God or deserve God. That's why bad things happen to good people and good things happen to bad people. There is no exchange system you can figure out. The smartest of us are puppies who understand 150 words. God is infinite. God is so beyond our understanding that the term beyond inherently implies our lack of faculties needed to understand an incomprehensible person with thoughts, feelings and actions not fixed by dimension. Where we see only in 123, 123 is a scratch & sniff sticker in the mind of God remembered fondly beyond beyonds ago. "Ago" being a limitation I'm trying to outdo in symbols pinned to a people in place & time, ingesting this at varying degrees of process capacity.

But anyway, I ended up on this beach trying to reach God. I was a child but that's how God wants us. Now, when I shit on the rug I hope that God thinks it's funny. But back then, I thought I could pray hard enough and become magical and reach some level of spiritual purity. It's what I wanted, and it bothered the fuck out of me, that God wasn't paying attention at my beck & call. Didn't God see how good I was?

God's plans are not our plans, but we can't see that because we're limited. If you're lucky, you can grope along in the dark and not trip too hard over the log God set in your path to keep you from running towards disaster while most of us just curse logs for getting in our way.

Peep Hole

You need to be right because
Your whole identity is rooted
In this notion that you're enlightened
You can see the real truth
You may not be the smartest person in the world
But you're definitely smarter than the masses
And no you probly shouldn't say it
but you're special
A little more special
than the 8 billion people on this planet
or the billions that came before, not the most special, obviouslyBut...
Baby, your point of view is tiny and life is big
You're not so special that a germ you need a microscope to see can't kill you
You're not so smart that you've figured out some way to not have to shit in the morning

You're just a speck in a big dusty room
Crying about furniture

But please, continue…
Tell me all the secrets of the universe you've accrued
In day one of the revolution around and round

Keep No Pets

The people who are offended by my vegan rhetoric, pointing out that youth are killed for your convenience and preference, are the same people who are offended that children are killed by guns in schools and they're bothered that I equate the mammal human life as being equal to the mammal bovine life.

As if humans farmed to feed the capitalist world engine value their own lives more than a cow farmed to feed the capitalist world engine does. Because they think they're better. And humans are the masters of life on earth. And that is why the earth is in its current ecological and moral downturn. It's also the same reason racism, slavery and segregation exist. You think you're better and someone thinks they're better than you and so on etc. But please, point out just how I'm incorrect.

Infatuacide

I've been thinking. I may be far too focused on sex and to a lesser extent focused on a relationship. I don't know how to undo this. This want isn't something I've chosen, it's just there. Maybe I should make a conscious effort to move against it.
A lot of energy goes into it, A lot of thought.

When I become infatuated with someone it's consuming. And nothing may ever come of it. When I fall in love, it takes over everything. I've learned that my little Cupid's arrow compass may be a little wonky. When I move on the path I think leads to sex. The chance of me putting myself in a dangerous situation is high and neither of these are what I truly want. They're just wants that hijack me.

Having a partner means having a shared vision. But my vision is strong. It doesn't require a co-visionary. I'm pro-pleasure, pro-sex, pro-love, Pro-what makes you happy… But these should enhance one's life, not enslave it. "You can do whatever you want" does not consider that life is an ocean and you are not it's master. Giant ocean liners sink, surfers drown, and tiny fish never think once about this world that can kill you or me.

I'm going to try and be more consciously aware of where my energy is going. I think the word is "focused." I hope for joy and awareness on your journey as well.

My Private Uzbekistan

Rage is justified in the wake of The US Supreme Court's overturning of Roe v Wade. A lot of people just got slapped in the face with the notion that when the founding fathers wrote the framework of government for this country, "by the people for the people" means that wealthy white landowners are people and everyone else is beneath them.

This has always been a labor colony built on a graveyard. In case you're unaware, the logos that formed this great nation is called manifest destiny, which means that anything that stands in the way of this place being as big as it can be, will be slaughtered.

When slavery ended; war, segregation, the war on drugs, and the penal system took its place. Guns are championed because they go hand in hand with crime. Which creates inmates, who provide jobs and labor. You will be livestocked however possible. You will be slotted into a stall where you will produce and consume, transferring energy and power to whoever may be running the farm.

Of course you're forced to breed. When you go against the policy framework that guides livestock towards energy output, drastic measures will be taken.

When Ghandi, led India to stop buying salt, just salt, it shook the British empire in South Asia. So, in no way am I saying that change is impossible. Change is possible.... in so much as it's required to keep the livestock producing.

If this were a country for the *people* people, you and me, we'd have funding for education and healthcare.... instead of war. We'd have something like a universal basic income. Isn't it crazy that the notion of NOT WORKiNG in this country is looked at as treacherous, that free education and free healthcare is called socialism, the dirtiest word Americans know. It's just that our point of view is really small ya know. We don't really know too much about the rest of the world because we have to work, or we die.

Anyway, enjoy the sun and the sky and the grass in the fields. Peace friends.

Tax the Church

I'm in the bath, thinking. Do you mind if I blabber? I'm more comfortable typing than speaking.

Like most of us, a lot of things are bothering me lately. The Supreme Court's overturning of Rowe vs Wade is something a lot a lot a lot of Christians wanted for a long time. I'm Christian. I used to be a Sunday school teacher. I went to college to study to be a missionary. My connection to god is the biggest part of my life. I also follow the teachings of Jesus to the best of my ability. I try anyway.

The church that I see, really looks nothing like a group of people following Christ's teachings. Christ was all about love and kindness and hated hypocrisy. He hated associating the church with money so much that he whipped those who were doing so with a belt. He was a radical. So radical he turned the world on its head.

He didn't try to control the world around him. He taught mostly just a small group of people.

I'm vehemently against the Christian culture of the United States. God does not need defending. God doesn't even want us defending ourselves. Christ taught that if someone hits you on one side, let them hit the other side too. Not, stockpile as many guns as you can.

White Republicanism is not Christianity. I'd go so far as to say that often it stands in direct opposition to the teachings of Christ. And I encourage anyone reading this to be well versed in both sides of socio-economic racism in its congruence to American Christianity. You might say, I don't have the time. You're going through it your whole life so you may as well be informed.

Secondly, I'm prosex. 99.999999999% of the world's human population comes from fucking. It's an innate part of life, like eating or sleeping. It's hardwired deep deep deep into all biology. So, it's weird to me that there's any stigma to it. It's weird that people are concerned with how anyone else does it or if they do it or not, or how they like it or who they like it with. It's a personal matter. Don't be an asshole about it.

Also, with regard to that matter, watching sex on tv is way less fucking weird to me than watching people get murdered. It's super fucking weird to me that people are casual about murder. It's horrific. That anyone can boo sex and yay murder is fucking weird. I've never killed anyone. I like to hope the overwhelming majority of people I know haven't killed anyone. But I'm pretty sure they've all had sex.

I don't like guns. I won't own guns. I don't want to touch guns. I would literally rather be killed than kill someone. I do think it's fine for someone to own a rifle or a handgun. They're not for me but I can see the argument for them. I do not see the argument for the proliferation of gun culture in this country. I do not see why anyone would need an assault rifle except to kill a bunch of people, because that's what it's made for. Just like a crack pipe is made for smoking crack.

I'm sorry. I wish I was better. I wish this country was better. I wish we treated each other with more kindness and more love and it's a fucking horrible thing for anyone to try and control other people. I'm vehemently against attacks on any personal freedom.

Did you know for the most part, you can't own a fucking bat or a lion in the United States, and there's not really any uproar about that. Because there's not a national fucking bat or lion association pumping billions of dollars into bureaucracy to make sure they can keep selling bats or lions.

Anyway, maybe have some ice cream and put on a nice song and enjoy the bath.
Cheerio,
Leon

Eighteen

Me personally, I like to think I can accept people regardless of what differences we may have. Relationships without differences are just masturbating.

I also am aware that I'm very particular. my views, personality, beliefs and upbringing, tend towards extremes, so I don't expect people to be like me and have for the most part just looked for the best in those I come across. I don't know if this is the best way. But this is what I do.

Occasionally, I've walked down a road with someone and realized that's about as far as I can go.

I'm amazed at people who look at someone and know they don't want to take that walk, cuz I won't know till we've gone aways.

The New Standardized Testing for Dummies

I think I'm going to start asking people how many books they've read on any given topic.

How many books have you read on American politics? How many books have you read on international politics? How many books have you read on biology or history? Any? Any at all?

If the answer isn't:

"I'm thoroughly informed on this topic and have an extensive understanding which I've acquired through vast reading and research on the topic."

or

"This is my life. I have immense experience in the field."

Then I'm going to assume that you have no idea what you're talking about. And probably just watched some videos or memes.

It's time we start calling stupid people stupid to their faces before this whole world falls apart.

Shelf Half Life

Perhaps we are the artificial god
As a computer is the artificial intelligence
Looking at it from that perspective
You would wonder what power you have in this life that you don't consider

ProLife or ProSelf?

People have become intrigued by the triviality of an artificial intelligence, a machine simulating thought. Well, here is the opposite of that. Human beings who've spent their life thinking about how they can bring life to you, how they can show or tell you from this extremely unique viewpoint, how they see life. In most cases, it's as if this is what they were born to do. They don't do it for money. It cost them usually everything they can afford to transform their internal energy into an outward manifestation on the rare chance that other humans will interact with them and hopefully something, however small, will have been added to their lives.

This Whole Entire System Exists Only to Take from You as Much As it Can

Practices promoting inclusivity lead to economic equality amongst peoples
Deteriorating an earmarked labor force
Promoting equality fosters freedom
Business doesn't want a free people
It doesn't want an educated people
It doesn't want a healthy people
Because not only are you working the farm
You're also being farmed for your earnings and energy
A people are maintained as livestock to provide
For the farmers
The landowners
The business

This is also why sexuality is under attack
If you're not breeding
You're not maintaining
The herd labor force
You serve no purpose to the farmer

Kill More CEOs

You're stuck on republican vs democrat
You're still waving an American flag
You're still defending an imaginary ideal
A place, a time that never existed
You're stuck in the lie
Playing by a set of rules
Given to the losers
By the winners
You're still calling this game great
And dying
Poor and feeble
Malnourished
Crying over the children killed in their classrooms
While the police waited outside
Unable to even keep track of school shootings
Anymore
Of mass shootings anymore
Of black and brown and poor young men
Killed in their cars by the police
No more
No more no more
No more
And I would like to end
But there's no end

Palawanian

I'd been in El Nido so long that that's what seemed like normal to me. My little room in the small hotel off a winding alley behind Marianna Suites. Walking up and down Hama Street 3x a day, dodging tuk-tuks and canines that don't care, jumping over muddy puddles. Drinking cheap bad instant coffee on my terrace and staring at the sea. Snaking into clothes that never dry and taking trips to beach towns hours away, as if I wasn't already on vacation and these weren't trips inside a trip. To get back to real life, I'd have to first get off this sand bar, then grab my backpack five hours away and catch a cramped van back to Puerto Princessa, fly to Manila, transfer to Hong Kong, and finally sneak back into Los Angeles and my apartment in Boyle Heights.

All of that seemed like seven cycles of reincarnation, being born again in economy class with the little pretzels and if I'm lucky no one sitting next to me. Real life was another galaxy and traveling light years seems so gross. Will LA even be there when I get back or will it have been burned down, sold off and liquidated by private equity to make room for slave labor immigration camps?

Ramen

A rise in abortions leads to a drop in crime
Less criminals
Less prisons
Less slave labor
Less guns sold
Less crimes
Less slave labor

As I continue to say,
The wealthy landowners this labor camp was
founded for persistently push practices
Which support a beholden labor force
Not a free people

Carnegiea Gigantea

I live in two places, right outside of downtown Los Angeles and a small desert town in Arizona. Arizona is always hard. It's a challenge. If I'm out here, it's for a reason. I don't come out here to chill. Usually I'm working on the house. I don't know anyone out here. It's kind of like living in a haunted house. Well, this is my dead dad's house but I don't mean it like that. If you ever lived in a haunted house, most of the time you just go about your life but at some point, you inevitably will be confronted with the ghost and you don't always get to choose how you react. Except here, the ghost is yourself. Here in the desert, in an empty house, it is inevitable that I will be forced to consider myself in ways I'd rather not. Am I a sex addict?
Am I a shitty person? Am I delusional? Am I trying? Am I in love with life? Am I giving enough?
Am I fucking someone over? Am I seeking out truth and love like a starving man? Am I complacent? Am I numb? Am I holding anyone captive to some unreachable prize for my own gain in any way? How much time do I have? Am I being understanding and forgiving? Is this rope tight enough to walk across? What next? If I stay out here will I become all dried out or does that only come from cigarettes? It's good to ask yourself questions but also good to answer them, move on and live your life. Thats all the space I have.

Leon McConnell

Fortune Cookies

95

Our limitations
Are most often placed
And reinforced by ourselves

93

Maybe just maybe
Every famous person is scum
And we've gone terribly astray
By worshipping them

94

Before every thought I spell out, know first that the unsaid context is I am an electron in the light before the sun all the way back to the creator who is the fire from which all light emanates.

82

All too often we get lost in the human parts of us that touch on chaos and despair
Forgetting that every cell of every step we inhabit borders on god

77

Love is waking up happy
You got to see them in your dreams

78

People who recline their seats on airplanes
Are the scum of the earth.

56

The triune godhead is expressed differently per dimension.

55

They're just people trying to be happy
Why do you hate them?

54

Do birds talk to ghosts?

59.

If you're more bothered by protests
Than suffering, you're a part of the problem

51

Love is wanting a person
To have their best
Even if it's not you

28

My heart's so full
I got enough blood to spill
And feed the wolves

26.

What cruel trick has life played on us
That so often
Wanting is better than having

69

"I have a smile for your lips."
Is the most polite way to say "come sit on my face."

1

Your worth is in your life
Not your production

-1

How silly it is to trick someone into giving you something you want

Look at you, you've managed a treat

Good boy

45

I want the most
...From myself

22

You're in love with me for the ride
And mad at me for kicking you off the bus
But it's my bus

30

I dreamed I set a fire
And woke up waiting for it to burn

2

Logic is understanding in a lower gear

3

The way you love me is like a kiss with teeth

4

Intuition is god talking back

5

Get to know a person
That is your tiny corner of god

6

Not only will you keep repeating your mistakes
Till you learn the lesson life has for you
You will repeat your actions

7

We can observe a dog's behavior
And can understand
Often why it behaves the way it does
But we rarely see people
As simply as we see dogs

8

Why would anyone want to live forever?
Another 20 years seems exhausting

9

This freedom of being untethered
Is so savage
We may as well be howling at the moon out here

10

Is the magic in the youth or the ignorance?
A wise elder will never know

62

Strung out on sex chemicals
A knife pushed through the sternum
A deep sigh

1991

Man continually wants to explain God
When God is unexplainable
So people feel that God fails us
When in reality words fail us

Oblivion is the Sweetest Darkest Nothing

If poverty is the gauntlet to be run
Opportunity is the rope ladder of corpsed hope
The husking exit to talon out and upwards
Raining broken trophies down
On the starving and the meek
Hope feeds
But few exit

1993

Your life is where you invest
In whom you invest it
Some life spending is for the now
Some is for later
And some is just a bad investment

Leon McConnell

Thirst Traps for Sadness

Break-up Letter One

Hi XXXXXX,

I know I should be saying this instead of writing it but my throat hurts. Sorry. I don't want to keep fighting to convince you I like you. I don't want to defend me just being me. But you being you seems to necessitate that. I don't want someone to follow me into a room and talk at me when I don't feel good (even if they have nice or interesting things to say.)

I'm happy by myself. I'm at peace by myself. I thought I could make my life better by adding someone to that. Someone I find hot and funny and smart and talented and that I have amazing sex with, someone who cares. Sadly, I don't think that's the case with you and I.
I don't think we work well in this area of life.
I wish me just wanting peace didn't make you feel bad or think horrible things. Sadly, I know it will.
I don't ever say this because I don't want to cause even more problems, but I need my peace. I'm not a perfect person. I have real problems. If I live life in this agitated state, my life won't last very long.
So, I hate that this will make you feel bad, but I need to protect myself.

I know you have anxiety, and you need to talk things through, but it's too much for me to deal with. I'm sorry.

I really wish I could just be this wave of love and affection to you that I'm trying to be and not anything that crashes or drowns.

To hear you talk about the bad ways I make you feel sounds horrible. You sound so oppressed by me and made to worry by me . I don't want to make you worry anymore. I guess I officially need to say
That I'm exiting this relationship. Which sucks
Because I think you're a great person
And that's what I want
That's why I've been here
That's why I deal with everything
Even though it's hard.
You're a truly great person
I don't want to stand in your way
I'm going to send you some money.
Maybe it will help with the hurt. I hope it does
Go to the job interview tomorrow
Go to the drs appointment on Friday
Return my birthday present.

I don't want to spend hours talking about this
I don't want to change my mind
I'm sorry to do such a hurtful thing.
I love you and I love your puppies.

But I need to protect my peace.

Sending you money via Zelle
Leon

Brick

I feel like I lost something very special
And yeah I made that decision
But I also feel that it was necessary
For my own health and safety
To create room for myself
Because my peace was under fire

Trick

I'm sad. I spent more than the last year of my life with someone, wrapping ourselves around each other in every way, merging. At times it was horrible, and I hated it. But I love this person, and I feel like a tooth has been pulled where my heart speaks, this ache of missing them where they were once a vital part of me.

-6

I don't enjoy being dissected
And then also made to feel bad
for saying I didn't enjoy it

Florist

I don't want the flowers growing at the edge of your tide pool in emotional turmoil

Zero

I don't want to be understood
I just want to be

Gripped

I've been wrestling with love
A love that holds on like dead hands
Bringing you back to the water
This isn't a struggle I'm made for
And I would rather die
Than fight with someone I care about
On a daily basis

Bone

Let's just have peace baby
No need to beg
Being close to you was the kick
Now all closeness looks like a leg

Flux

When your energy goes
to explaining yourself
And defending yourself
That's less power you have
For being yourself

Written in the Margins

Here I am sitting, thinking about XXXXXX. I care for her. I want her to succeed. I want the best version of her to walk through her life.
And I wonder, what can I do for her still?
What can I give her? How can I help?
I could give her my love. My true love, all of it.
But.... I did. And she didn't accept it. She sniffed at it. She picked it up. She even held it sometimes. But she couldn't stop poking at it, turning it over, kicking it around to see how it works. So, I took my love back and I can't give it like that again. Not to her.
Maybe not to anyone, sadly.

Post Adolescent Drama

It's hard words to spell out
That I'm trying to keep the dark from closing in
& you seem to love throwing the curtains shut
So I have to do the hard work and push the knife between our twined-up fingers
Somebody's gunna lose a pinkie, I'm sure
And I have to push away
Leave my heart
Abandon the suitcase full of quarters
I sunk into playing this game with you
At some point I thought we'd play forever
But you smoke in the arcade
And the smoke makes me sick

That's reason enough
How'm I suppose to want to meet anyone
When I know everyone walking past
Is just walking past
When you were sex in the doorway
And a laugh on the steps
Chaos waiting under charm
So well spoken
I don't really want to play anymore
I'm already caught up in keeping
The dark from closing in
Life is game enough

Trot

I didn't run off
I didn't leave you to run wild
I wanted you to run with me
But neither of us could run
As long as I was carrying you
I tried to make it so we'd walk hand in hand
But you stood there crying
Too long to catch up
Thats not really side by side
And the road just took me away
I guess I started running at some point
Because I felt free
And that felt good

Paring Knife

Being in love is sad. It doesn't always work with what's best for you. Sometimes even, being in love can be bad for you. It could even be the worst thing for you.

This person you gave your most to, this person you had the most with, the most fun, the deepest talks, the best sex, this person you're closest to, your best friend…. Can wreck you. You can let them wreck you a hundred times, a thousand times. But you only have so many wrecks left. They can break you.

It's your job to not let yourself be broken. They could be the funniest, the smartest, the most talented. But when they stick that knife in your side… you bleed you scar. And it's a pretty knife. They've grafted onto it apologies and compliments and sometimes they stab you in the softest ways. Still the knife goes in.

You've grown used to it. You let them stab you a little, if it means you can get out…. Of the way from the mania, the sandstorm, the labyrinth, the cloud. When madness hits them they pin you in and stab and the knife is wielded in tears. Question after question. No answer will save you. All you can hope for is a pool of soul blood to float away in.

So you scream, stop stop please stop. Please stop. Please don't do this. Please stop. What just happened? We were having so much fun. But all they see is you holding a knife, attacking them with a mirror. In your defense they see an abuser. In your begging for relief they see a monster.

Walk away. Do every hard thing. Everything will be so hard. But walk away. Never come back to them. Never let them come back. You'll die. Some way you'll die. This is love.

WereWolves

It's weird to be old and carry all this time in you so that sand makes you think of desert roads. Driving next to someone you've loved and or love still. Their leg wrapped in bandage from a burn they got three days before Christmas when things went poorly between you because they woke up in a bad mood and you're sick of someone giving you shit for sleeping. She cried in the toilet and you let her cry because you value privacy and she wondered why anyone would ever let her cry because she values people getting involved. This old stretch of highway reminds you of that because you went to that CVS to get her the silver sulfadiazine your cousin prescribed and now that burn is just a scar on her tattoos that makes you a little sad every time you see it because you think no one needs to hurt like that.

Being old means any given memory can hit you like this in any given place because sand is everywhere and dust is in everything and you've been to so many beaches, touched so many bodies, burned under so many suns, just one sun. It never lets go, just gives you nights off but the nights are cold. I've seen the moon out so many windows and fallen asleep while driving but those memories are all my own. There's no one to love in them but me. So many nights I carry with me.

The Truth is the Truth no Matter How Anyone Sees It

Do you ever wonder if you did it wrong? I mean, maybe you put in an honest effort but in the end, your design failed.

Am I at fault for binding with someone who actually offered some sort of love, a storm, a pain, a madness, but a love still. Am I wrong because that's the love I identified as for me. Maybe there were other ones, less erratic loves. But it seems they were outside of my visible spectrum. Maybe I'm too limited. Maybe I'm colorblind and can't see the red flags. They just looked like wings to me, and I so badly wanted to watch you fly.

Maybe this is the way it was supposed to go. Some pain for you, some pain for me and everyone goes through life all the more tolerant, resistant, deeper, stronger, with perhaps a greater depth of field that can only be gained through a wound. Maybe I fucked up. Maybe I'll die alone in the dust like my dad did, loved only in dementia. Maybe I won't take so many more gambles.

Maybe if nothing else I've learned I'm not indestructible and up for any car crash if it means we have the most fun for a minute. Maybe growing up means accepting your fragility. Even tanks are allergic to land mines I suppose.

Maybe I'll watch this gash scar and fade till it's just a pretty pink line. Maybe I have enough scars now. Maybe I'm complete.

Untouchable you

I feel haunted by a human being who lives
Just a few miles away
If haunted means stuck
If haunted means horrible
If haunted means putting in my best
And becoming my worst
If haunted means unstable
And horribly horribly frustrated
I feel haunted by someone I've cared for deeply
Someone who I feel loved me
And that I loved back
Someone I saw great traits in
I feel haunted
If haunted means life teetering on madness
towards destruction
I feel haunted
By a mind that amazed me from time to time
By sex that is most likely the best I've ever had
I feel haunted by someone who made me laugh
But more often made me feel like shit

Break up Letter Number Two

Hi XXXXXX,

I said I'd think about you and I, and that's what I've done. Nothing but think. I don't need several days. I'm sure by then I'll hurt less. I'd rather just go through all the hurt and not start a fresh batch.

I know that on any occasion you and I could spend time together and be happy and there'd be so many good things. Any day. And then at some point things will go bad and I'll feel like shit. I don't know the exact percentage differential between times you make me feel good and times you make me feel like shit. But it's not one that I can accept.

I don't need to insult or investigate you or weigh the scales between us or demand some justice. I just want to not feel like shit. I'm so traumatized by this experience. I'm sure I'll hear your voice interrogating and accusing me for far too long, pushing me, wanting me to acknowledge that I'm bad. I've never called you crazy but that's a crazy thing to do.

I truly honestly only wanted to make you happy. I don't know why you would attack someone who just wants to make you happy. But you attacked me over and over again, maybe not every day. Maybe not every other day but that's about as far as I can go on that and still maintain accuracy.

Leon McConnell

I'm sorry. I'm sorry for dragging this out. I should've severed the ties between us a very long time ago. There are so many good things about you though. You make it easy to write off an argument, no matter how heated they get. But all those arguments wound my soul.
I'd like to not feel bad anymore please. You aren't someone I can keep in my life.

I'm in awe of your talent and sometimes your insight and always where you know you're number one.
I hope you find good things that make you happy.
I hope your new job goes well. I hope xxxx has many healthy years left in him. I'm very happy your children became my friends.

This letter sounds bad. It truly is a goodbye. Please respect that. Please don't pester me. I'm hurt enough. Just move on with your life and let me move on with mine. We have no plans. We have no sex. We have no friendship. All that is gone.

You loved me and I loved you and those are the things we had. It'd definitely make an exciting movie if God is watching with a bucket of popcorn.

I have your lil white suitcase. I'm going to give it back to you. I don't want it. I have a bunch of your other stuff. I can hold that and give it to you when you want it. But it's mostly in Arizona so you'll need to let me know in advance.

Bye XXXXXXXXX.
Love Leon.

Break Up Letter Number Three

Hi XXXXXX,

I'm going to try and be short here.
You've been my closest person, my best friend, my heart, my greatest collaborator
And my hardest challenge.

Thats a lot. It's very much.
 It's very extreme.

But I don't think you've been honest with me.
I mean between you and god cuz I know you'll never tell me, how many lies have you told me?
How many lies would there be if I knew what to ask?

I'm going to pull out. I'm going to go away and give up. You've been all these things. You've been so much to me. But I can't be anything to you anymore. It costs me too much of myself. I feel so stupid for trying so hard with you. I feel used.

I'm sorry if this is dramatic. I don't think it has ever really needed to be. I guess that's just the way we are.

You should cancel your work week off. I'm going to cancel the hotel. I've tried really hard. I just don't think we'll ever be anything. And that's ok. You're over there. Make a good life. Do great things. I can't sacrifice myself anymore to have something with you.

Sorry to be annoying. This is the last of all the things.

A piece of my heart will probably always be yours.
Love Leon

PS
Thanks for being my love
Despite all the hurt between us
I'm happy we got to have that

Sarcastic and Mean

Life is to be accepted
Experienced
Lived
Not understood
Or disseminated
Enjoy
Feel
Live
Maybe
Someday
Someone
Will say this
In a podcast
And you'll
Finally
Believe it
But I'll be gone
By then

Return Ticket

Sadness will claim you
And take you back home
To lock you away

Belly

I am not calm
I am not happy
I'm surrounded by this opulent
extravagant intense beauty
But the balance in my soul is off
The mouth in my heart is starving
The cavern at the bottom of my sea is void
And I feel like I could suck it all in
Spare the world that
The smallest taste could satisfy
But I don't know the taste of what
These scales have no discernment
I just want
More and more

Not the Stinging Ash Blowing Past Your Cheek

Everyone I know is just a drawing on the wall
Scrubbed out and faded from my life
I walk through this quiet city
Misted, Gone by 11am

Leon McConnell

Black Salt Circle

When I've cut off my hands
And the sword has been pushed deep down
When blood and bits or liver choke and spittle
I will cough satisfied
I will have been perfected

Langston Hughes

I want someone to know that I'm depressed
That I'm deeply depressed and have been for years
I want someone to know that I'm lonely
That nothing seems to fix that
It's a celestial sized loneliness
With the gravity to suck bodies
Out of orbit
The people I reach out to for help
Most often don't
A lot of the time they make the issue worse
I don't know how to dig myself out of this
I don't know how to fill my problem
I keep trying to stabilize
Grabbing out for something to hold onto
But all I can reach is razors

Sargasso Sea

When you're sailing the great big sea of time, some days blow by, some days are busy, some ships are cruise ships and the week is a party. Some days you have a purpose. You're sailing to port, buying spices, drawing whales, texting mermaids. Somedays there's no wind. Some days your feet dangle over the side and the sun burns. The fish don't even take notice. The turtles have no interest in you. You call out to god and god answers. God says be alive. I gave you all this. But alive sometimes comes with no change. Alive sometimes is still, which is weird when you're at sea. Alive sometimes is a deep breath. How deep can you go? Sometimes we have to just be alive and breathe and when your breath has taken deep enough, deep as this tiny shallow sea, then your sail will take that breath and you will slowly move back into the currents of life, all the more appreciative of when the world gives you turn.

Leon McConnell

The End

I Am
Hungry
Lonely
Starving
But No
Not You

Dark Knights

I'm not an artist. I'm fucking heartless and the shit I say, I'd say regardless …of who hears because I'm not expressing myself, I'm an express jet falling on def ears and my rhyme patterns are blood spattered napkins, scattered thrashings I spat em in between nappings. In dreams, I worship at the altar of a daughter who never bothered to please her father or pull her halter top down. I didn't try to stop her. I judged her by the cover and read her all across town. In night gowns and on freeways, under duvets, I prayed to a God that lives inside thighs. Heaven is where I come from and every time I come back I die a little bit inside but what's it matter. The world turns and I'ma take mine, I'ma drag fuck all by my teeth like a tow line. To each their own and I've grown mine, out of pure will but there's a hole in my heart and it can't be filled. So, I'm throwing bodies in it like we got 59 seconds to live. Give me a minute. I'll spend it sinning. And in a second my head'll have you spinning. It's a dirty mind. There ain't no time for that but you're such a pretty thang. These other motherfuckers cant hang. They're stars from a crescent moon while I'm going big bang!

Crumble

Yo, this is a shout out, if you're listening. I'm fading to these city lights like a moth dissipating and my def rhymes they fall on deaf ears. Like whispers in a dream they bounce off pillows but still I spill those guts ..And even if this cuts the deepest I can't keep sleeping. There's more sheep than I could ever even count out here. And I'm trying to amount to something but the pressure's mounting and my friends they're sitting on the slope of it pouting.
I don't have hope. I have work. Mount Rushmore couldn't come any faster. So plaster my head over the dead and fallen. Yeah, I got an open mind and I want you to crawl in. Come inside, take a look. I got a place that you can hide from the search. My thoughts are earth. My thoughts are dirt. And just because you can't hear this planet cry doesn't mean it doesn't hurt.

I'ma start at the end, get cold, dig a hole and fuck the world with my soul, press send and spend eternity burning ear drums till the lord comes. You can catch me wrecking words like I stole them. I remember when, you wrote me off before I could even find a pen or comprehend what makes men. It's embracing a struggle that you might not win, getting kicked in the nuts and having the guts to fight again. It's shitting on a friend, stealing the flowers from his grave, calling up his wife and giving her all those fucks you never gave. Like I care. I'm not human. I'm a freak. I'ma slave to this beat. I'm aware of each and every stare so listen while I throw my middle fingers in the air cuz I want y'all to fuck off and kiss feet.

Invisible

Yo, I woke up
And South Gate is the Labyrinth
I know shit went down with some white rabbits
But how the fuck I fall in this hole full of bad habits
Wishing that a break would go my way
like Lenny Kravitz
Yo, kids are shooting
And time moves on
Your friends are in prison
The days are long
The nights stay short
And I can't sleep with no-one
Unless I know they'll abort
The mission is no commonsense
And all my dreams is dead like these presidents
I'ma do what I do and you can say what you want
And I'ma do what I do and you can say what you want And I'ma do what I do
Yeah, that's true
I got cans to rack
I got busses to kill

Leon McConnell

I got a tap card man
And I still ride the grill
I know I make it look easy

I'm not invisible
I'm not invisible
I'm not invisible
So don't act like you don't see me

Graveyard shift is a mother fucking bitch
I'm just trying to pay rent
I ain't trying to get rich
All these rappers in the club
While I'm freezing off my dick
Cuz I made 100 songs
And ain't one of them a hit
Do what I do
And you can say what you wanted
But the body is a temple and my house is fucking haunted
Kids are shooting Tik-Toks in the street
And all my friends moved on, they forgot about me
I ain't one of them fuckers
that can live, love, laugh so easily
I love what I got
and I would never say I'm miserable
I guess I'm just a solitary individual

I'm not invisible
Oh, I'm not invisible

Fuchlestichs

I ain't a safe haven
I spit fire and stay hating
Don't wait, there ain't no placating
Life is math and I'm in love with the equation
While you other motherfuckers settled for a mate and a PlayStation
I did what I did and I said what I said
And if I make it to old age, I'll still end up dead
I got hips to break
I got pills to pop
Still run them red lights man
Fuck the cops
Kids are swooping past me at full speed
Nobody cares who I used to be
I was the king of bust
I rhymed anything man
Time still brings the dust
And now I'm just milenia-ing
It's hard breathing every syllable
But I keep my heart breathing out of principle

I'm not invisible
I'm not invisible
I'm not invisible

www.ingramcontent.com/pod-product-compliance
Lightning Source LLC
Chambersburg PA
CBHW060205050426
42446CB00013B/2995